99 WAYS
NOT TO BECOME A
GRUMPY
OLD LADY

This book belongs to

_____

Table of Contents

Your Anti-Grump Survival Guide

At some point in life, every woman faces the same dangerous crossroads. On one side: becoming that bitter old lady who yells at kids for stepping on her lawn, complains about everything from the weather to the neighbors and spends her days collecting grudges like trophies. On the other side: staying bold, funny, curious and just a little bit legendary. This book exists to make sure you choose the second road.

The truth is, aging doesn't turn you into a grump. Bad habits do. A lack of laughter, saying yes when you want to say no, stressing about things that don't matter, comparing yourself to everyone else, punishing yourself instead of enjoying life: That's how bitterness sneaks in. But here's the good news... it's completely avoidable.

What you're holding in your hands is not a lecture and definitely not a boring self-help manual. It's a collection of 99 playful reminders, practical tricks and cheeky challenges designed to keep you lighthearted instead of heavy, vibrant instead of bitter. Think of it as your anti-grump guide: a funny little companion that nudges you toward joy when the world tries to drag you toward misery.

These pages will not tell you to be perfect, patient or saintly. Instead, they'll tell you to dance in your kitchen, take naps without guilt, forgive but not forget, declutter your chaos and laugh so hard you scare the cat. They'll remind you that kindness beats competition, that inspiration is everywhere and that your best stories are still waiting to be written.

So buckle up. Whether you're in your thirties, forties, sixties or beyond, this book is here to prove one thing: you don't have to become a bitter old lady. You can become something far better. You can become unforgettable. Are you ready?

Mindful Mornings, Calmer Days

Mindful Mornings, Calmer Days:
How small choices set the tone

Mornings decide more than people want to admit. They create the rhythm for everything that follows and once the first hour of your day slips into stress, it feels almost impossible to catch up again. Think about how often your day begins with a race against the clock: you oversleep, rush into the shower, throw on clothes that do not feel right and bolt out the door with a coffee cup clutched in your hand like it is the only thing keeping you upright. No wonder the smallest delay (a missing key, a late bus, a spilled drink) feels like a disaster. The truth is, mornings do not have to be this way. A calm start is not a luxury for people with easier lives, it is a conscious choice you can practice. Creating a routine that slows the pace, even just slightly, changes not only your mood but your capacity to handle what the day throws at you. When you choose order and calm first thing in the morning, you are setting the foundation for resilience, focus and a lighter spirit that lasts long after the coffee cup is empty.

"Either you run the day or the
day runs you."
– Jim Rohn

1. Prep the night before

The first step to a calm morning is not what you do when the alarm rings, but what you do the evening before. Ten minutes of preparation at night can transform your entire next day. Lay out your clothes, pack your bag and check that breakfast and coffee are ready to go. When you wake up, instead of scrambling half-asleep, you simply follow the plan you created. It feels like giving your tired morning-self a gift from the night before. You skip three unnecessary decisions and remove three potential points of stress before they even appear. This habit, small as it seems, creates the feeling that you are already one step ahead of the day. Preparation is not about perfection, it is about kindness to your future self.

2. Skip the snooze button

The snooze button pretends to be your friend, but it is really a thief. It promises you more rest, but what it delivers is shallow, unsatisfying sleep that makes you even more tired. Each time you press it, your brain dips in and out of confusion and when you finally drag yourself up, you feel groggy, rushed and behind. Instead, set your alarm for the actual time you need to wake up and place it out of reach. When it rings, stand up immediately and let movement do the rest. Within a few minutes, your body adjusts and you feel more alert than if you had stolen those fragmented extra minutes. The discipline to get up on the first ring is like a small win before the day even begins and that sense of control spreads into everything else you do. Snoozing feels good for a moment, but rising on time feels good for the whole day.

3. Coffee before emails

Nothing derails a calm morning faster than opening your inbox before you have even taken a sip of coffee. The moment you check your phone, you hand over your attention to other people's demands. Suddenly you are pulled into their schedules, their problems, their urgency. And your own morning disappears. Protecting the first half-hour of your day is an act of self-respect. Brew your coffee (or tea), sit down and drink it with intention. Let the ritual of warmth, smell and taste ground you before the world intrudes. Only once you feel anchored should you glance at messages or emails. The difference in stress level is immediate and striking. You move from reactive to proactive, from scattered to centered. Your inbox can wait, but your peace of mind cannot.

4. Add one happy ritual

Mornings are often treated as a gauntlet to survive, but they can also be a chance to create joy. Adding one small ritual changes the emotional tone of the entire day. Play your favorite song while you make breakfast. Light a candle as you get ready. Write down one thing you are looking forward to. Even a one-minute stretch can feel like a declaration that the morning belongs to you. These small actions act like anchors for your mood, reminding you that life is not only about what you have to do, but also about what you choose to enjoy. Over time, these rituals build into habits that protect you from slipping straight into stress. A happy ritual, no matter how small, is proof that you are allowed to start the day on your own terms.

Just Say No Without Guilt

Just Say No Without Guilt:
Boundaries that feel like freedom

For many women the hardest word in the world is the shortest one ("no"). From childhood on we are taught to be polite, to keep the peace and to put the needs of others first. Teachers praise the helpful student, parents reward the obedient child and society applauds women who carry every burden without complaint. The result is a habit of agreement that follows us into adult life and quietly drains us. Every time you agree to something you do not want, you give away your time, your focus and a piece of your peace of mind. Over months and years that pattern builds into exhaustion, resentment and a creeping sense of losing yourself. The irony is that saying no is rarely as dramatic as you fear. Most people accept it quickly, sometimes with more respect than when you give in. A clear no is kinder than a reluctant yes because it sets honest boundaries instead of planting silent frustration. Boundaries are not rejection, they are a declaration of self-respect. When you begin to say no without guilt you discover that you are not closing doors but opening space for what you truly value. No is not an attack, it is an act of care for yourself and, in the long run, for everyone around you.

"No is a complete sentence."
– Anne Lamott

5. Saying no means saying yes to yourself

Every no is also a hidden yes. When you refuse something that drains you, you make room for something that restores you. Think of the evenings you have spent at events you dreaded, the favors you agreed to out of obligation, the projects you accepted when you were already overwhelmed. Each one stole energy that could have gone to rest, to joy or to work that really mattered. By saying no, you buy back your own life. You give yourself permission to rest without apology, to create without interruption and to spend time where it counts. A constant stream of yeses leaves nothing left for you and when you collapse, everyone around you feels it too. Protecting your energy allows you to show up better for the commitments you actually choose.

6. You do not owe anyone a long explanation

Many people imagine that a refusal needs a long story, as if only a convincing excuse makes it valid. In truth no is enough on its own. You do not have to pile on apologies or invent reasons that make your answer sound acceptable. When you add endless explanations, you weaken your boundary and invite negotiation. Simple sentences such as "That does not work for me" or "I cannot commit to that right now" are both polite and final. They communicate your decision clearly without opening the door to persuasion. The more you practice short, firm refusals, the easier it becomes to trust them. Clarity is kinder than confusion and most people appreciate honesty even if they are momentarily disappointed. Your time is valuable and you do not need to defend every choice you make.

7. Boundaries are self-respect in action

It is easy to talk about self-care in vague terms, but boundaries are where the theory becomes real. Saying yes when you want to say no teaches you that your own needs are negotiable, while everyone else's are absolute. Over time that belief erodes confidence and fuels resentment. Boundaries reverse the lesson. They show that your time and attention are limited resources that deserve protection. When you set a boundary, you are not shutting people out, you are teaching them how to treat you. Strong relationships depend on realistic expectations, not endless sacrifice. If you respect yourself enough to draw a line, others will learn to respect it too. Boundaries may feel uncomfortable at first, but they create the conditions for healthier, more balanced connections.

8. Stop apologizing every time you say no

Apologies are meant for mistakes, not for boundaries. Yet many people begin every refusal with "I am sorry," as if protecting their own time were an offense. This habit turns a strong no into a weak one and leaves you sounding guilty for something you have the right to do. Replace apology with gratitude. Instead of "Sorry, I cannot," try "Thank you for thinking of me." This small change flips the tone from shame to appreciation, while keeping your answer clear. It shows that you can decline with respect and still honor the other person's effort. Over time the habit of guilt-free refusals transforms how you see yourself. You stop treating your limits as failures and start seeing them as proof of strength.

Self-Love Beats Self-Criticism

Self-Love Beats Self-Criticism:
Kindness to yourself changes everything

Most women speak to themselves in ways they would never use with a friend. One glance in the mirror and the mind starts listing flaws. A small mistake at work and the inner voice repeats it for days as if it defined your whole worth. This habit of criticism is so common that many believe it is normal, but constant self-judgment drains confidence and joy. It keeps you from taking risks, from celebrating progress and from enjoying the person you already are. Real change begins not with harsher discipline but with softer words. Self-love is not arrogance, it is the foundation for resilience. It allows you to stand up again after failure, to keep trying even when progress is slow and to enjoy the life you are living instead of waiting for perfection. Without it, every achievement feels too small and every mistake feels too large. With it, mistakes become lessons and successes become reasons to celebrate. The way you talk to yourself writes the script for your entire life. Change the words and you change the story.

"You yourself, as much as anybody in the entire universe, deserve your love and affection." - Buddha

9. Talk to yourself like a best friend

Imagine your closest friend comes to you in tears after a difficult day. You would never call her stupid, lazy or unworthy. You would remind her of her strengths, her efforts and the times she has overcome challenges before. Now compare that compassion to how you treat yourself in similar situations. Most people reserve kindness for others and direct their harshest words inward. Begin by noticing this pattern and gently correcting it. When you catch yourself thinking, "I failed again," replace it with, "I am learning." When you hear, "I look terrible," answer with, "I am taking care of myself." Over time these small shifts reshape the tone of your inner voice. The more you practice, the more natural kindness becomes, until your default reaction is support rather than sabotage.

10. Write down three wins every day

Your mind is designed to highlight what went wrong, not what went right. This negativity bias was useful for survival in the past, but in daily life it keeps you stuck on failures. Combat it by creating a written record of small victories. Each night, write down three things you did well. They do not have to be extraordinary. Maybe you handled a task you had postponed, cooked a healthy meal or stayed calm when you could have snapped. By recording these moments, you train your brain to notice progress instead of only problems. With time, this journal becomes a library of proof that you are capable and growing. On difficult days you can flip back and see pages filled with evidence that you are more resilient than you feel.

11. Celebrate progress, not perfection

Perfection is an unreachable target that steals joy from every achievement. Even when you succeed, the critical voice says it was not enough or points out what you could have done better. To escape this trap, shift your focus from perfect outcomes to steady improvement. Notice the moments when you react with more patience than before, when you complete a task faster than last time or when you find the courage to start something new. These are the signs that you are moving forward. Celebrate them as victories. Progress builds confidence and momentum, while perfectionism only builds frustration. By honoring progress, you allow yourself to feel joy in the journey instead of punishing yourself for not yet reaching an impossible standard.

12. Compliment yourself out loud

There is surprising power in hearing your own voice speak kindly. Silent thoughts can be dismissed, but spoken words sound more real, more permanent. Each time you say, "I handled that well," or "I look good today," your brain records it as truth. At first, you may cringe or laugh, but persistence transforms the practice. Choose one compliment a day, no matter how small and say it aloud. Over weeks, you will notice that these words shape your self-image in subtle ways. The awkwardness fades and the compliments start to feel deserved. Eventually, you begin to believe them without effort, because your brain has accepted kindness as normal. This practice not only lifts your mood in the moment, it rewires your inner voice for the long term.

Embrace Digital Detox Days

Embrace Digital Detox Days:
Scroll less, live more

Modern life is built around screens. From the moment the alarm rings until the last minutes before bed, many people are scrolling, swiping and staring at glowing rectangles. It feels normal, yet the constant flood of information slowly steals attention, focus and calm. Instead of enjoying meals, people photograph them. Instead of resting, they check notifications. Hours disappear into feeds that leave you neither wiser nor happier. This habit is not harmless. It shapes your brain, your relationships and even your sense of self. Reclaiming your attention does not mean rejecting technology, but learning to use it on your own terms. A digital detox is not a punishment but a gift, a reminder that your life exists beyond the screen. When you create space without constant digital noise, you notice details you had forgotten: the sound of your own breathing, the warmth of your coffee, the calm of silence. The more often you disconnect, the more you realize that the best parts of life rarely happen on a screen.

"The price of anything is the amount of life you exchange for it."
– Henry David Thoreau

13. Turn off notifications for one day

Notifications train your brain to live in a state of constant alert. Each ping suggests urgency, even when the message is trivial and over time your attention becomes fragmented into tiny pieces. Turn everything off for one full day and observe the difference. At first you may reach for your phone out of habit and feel a wave of unease, but that feeling fades as your nervous system quiets down. You start and finish tasks without interruption, conversations feel deeper and your thoughts stretch out instead of breaking every few minutes. It is surprising how quickly clarity returns when your pocket stops buzzing. By the evening you will likely realize that almost nothing truly required an instant response and you will be tempted to leave many alerts off permanently.

14. No-phone meals taste better

Eating while scrolling robs a simple ritual of its joy. Your brain splits focus between food and feed and you end up satisfied by neither. Commit to phone-free meals for a week. Sit down, take a breath and notice the smell and heat of the plate in front of you. If you are with others, let the conversation meander without the constant tug to check a screen. If you are alone, pay attention to flavors, textures and the pace of your chewing, because mindful eating actually helps your body register fullness. After a few days, mealtimes begin to feel like small islands of calm inside a busy day and the urge to document everything fades. A meal enjoyed with full attention nourishes more than hunger, it repairs your focus.

15. Swap bedtime scrolling for a book

Nighttime scrolling pretends to be relaxation, but it keeps your brain alert long past the point when you need rest. Blue light delays melatonin, the endless feed pushes novelty and your thoughts keep racing even after you put the phone down. Replace the habit with twenty minutes of reading or a calm audio story. Dim the lights, slow your breathing and let your eyes rest on steady lines of text rather than flashing images. The first nights may feel strange, yet within a week most people fall asleep faster and wake up clearer. Sleep debt shrinks, mood stabilizes and mornings start with more patience. Entertainment that steals tomorrow's energy is not worth tonight's distraction. Choose the ritual that restores you instead of the one that drains you.

16. One unplugged hour a day keeps stress away

Pick an hour and treat it as sacred time. Morning, lunch or evening works as long as you are consistent. Put your phone in another room and choose one simple activity: a walk, gentle stretching, cooking, journaling or even doing nothing on purpose. The first minutes may itch with habit, but a quiet rhythm soon appears. Your attention stops jumping, your shoulders loosen and ideas arrive that never show up while you are scrolling. After a few weeks this hour becomes a refuge you look forward to rather than a rule you fight. A single hour of true presence can rebalance an entire day of noise. You return to your devices with clearer priorities and a mind that feels like it belongs to you again.

Learn to Be Like a Cat

Learn to Be Like a Cat:
Elegance, calm and a touch of ignorance

Cats don't hustle. They don't apologize for naps. They don't care if you like them or not, and still, they somehow get fed, admired and endlessly photographed. That is the magic of being a cat: doing less, stressing less and demanding more comfort without guilt. Imagine applying even a fraction of that attitude to your life. How many headaches would vanish instantly? Cats choose softness over struggle, rest over constant rushing and elegance over chaos. Most of us have been trained to do the opposite. We rush, we overthink, we please everyone until we collapse. But maybe the secret to a lighter life is hiding in your living room, stretched out on the sofa with zero shame. A cat knows its worth without needing likes, approval or endless comparison. It does what feels good and ignores what doesn't. The lesson is simple: when in doubt, nap. When stressed, stretch. And when someone asks too much, give them the same look a cat gives when you dare move them from their spot.

"In ancient times cats were worshipped as gods; they have not forgotten this."
– Terry Pratchett

17. Nap without guilt

When a cat is tired, it lies down and closes its eyes. It does not check the clock, it does not wonder if it deserves a rest, it simply does it. This is a lesson worth borrowing. A nap is not wasted time but a reset for the mind and body. Ten to twenty minutes of rest can sharpen your memory, calm your nerves and lift your mood more effectively than another cup of coffee. Modern culture glorifies pushing through exhaustion, but exhaustion rarely leads to brilliance. By giving yourself permission to nap, you honor your limits and prevent burnout before it arrives. Think of it not as indulgence but as maintenance, the same way you charge your phone before the battery runs flat.

18. Ignore stupid people with elegance

Cats never waste time arguing with barking dogs. They lift their heads, flick their tails and walk away with elegance. This ability to disengage is one of their greatest strengths. Not every comment deserves your attention and not every provocation deserves your energy. People will always say foolish things, but that does not mean you have to respond. When you walk away, you keep your peace and send a silent message of strength. Silence, paired with dignity, is often louder than the sharpest comeback. The next time someone tries to bait you, imagine yourself as a cat who does not even hear the noise. You will notice how quickly your stress level drops when you refuse to play a game you never wanted to join. Nothing is more powerful than refusing to be dragged into nonsense. The people who matter will admire your composure rather than your ability to argue.

19. Walk into rooms like you own them

Cats do not sneak into spaces as if they need permission. They enter with poise, as if every room belongs to them and that confidence changes the way others treat them. You can cultivate the same presence. Stand tall, keep your chin lifted and move at a steady pace. Even if you feel uncertain inside, your body language will speak for you and people will respond as if you belong. Confidence is often an act first and a feeling second. By acting as though you are comfortable, you slowly train yourself to be comfortable. Over time, what began as a posture becomes genuine self-assurance. It isn't arrogance when you stand tall, it's simply presence. And presence makes every conversation smoother, every meeting easier, and every social moment more natural.

20. Stretch like it is your secret power

Cats stretch constantly and it keeps them graceful and agile. Most people, however, sit stiff at desks, walk with tense shoulders and forget that the body needs care as much as the mind. Adding a few minutes of stretching into your day changes everything. Loosen your spine after sitting, roll your shoulders to release pressure or lengthen your legs before bed. These small movements bring blood flow back into the muscles, ease stress and make you feel more awake. Stretching is a reset button you can press anytime. Just like cats use stretching to prepare for both rest and play, you can use it to prepare for work, exercise or simply to feel lighter in your own body. When you treat stretching as a daily ritual rather than an afterthought, you build flexibility in your body and resilience in your mind.

Stop Competing,
Start Complimenting

Stop Competing, Start Complimenting: Why supporting others makes life lighter

Comparison is a thief that quietly robs people of joy. One moment you feel proud of yourself, the next you see someone else with a nicer home, a slimmer figure or a more impressive job title and suddenly your pride shrinks. Social media has made this even worse, because it parades endless highlight reels and convinces you that everyone else is winning while you are standing still. The truth is that constant competition does not make you stronger, it makes you bitter. Complimenting others, on the other hand, lifts both sides. It does not take anything away from you to say, "You did a great job," but it adds warmth to your relationship and lightness to your own spirit. The more you celebrate others, the less space envy has to grow inside you. Confidence does not come from crushing competition, it comes from standing firmly in your own worth while lifting others up. Life feels lighter when you stop running imaginary races and start building real connections.

"Admire someone else's beauty without questioning your own."
- Unknown

21. Celebrate other women openly

Jealousy thrives in silence, while admiration grows when spoken out loud. If a colleague gives a sharp presentation, say so. If a friend looks stunning, tell her. These compliments may feel small, but they ripple outward. They make her day brighter and remind you that success is not limited. Someone else's brilliance does not mean you shine less. In fact, noticing beauty and strength in others helps you recognize them in yourself. Kindness spoken aloud is contagious, spreading warmth to places competition can never reach. Over time, celebrating others openly creates an environment where women support each other instead of silently resenting one another. That shift changes relationships, workplaces and even the way you view yourself in the mirror.

22. Avoid drama queens

Not everyone wants to leave competition behind. Some thrive on conflict, turning every interaction into a contest. They measure worth by who gets the last word or who attracts the most attention. If you let them, they will pull you into their endless battles. The strongest response is not to join the fight but to decline it. Walk away when conversations turn toxic. Change the subject when gossip begins. Protecting your peace is more valuable than proving a point. Elegance in walking away shows more strength than shouting ever could. When you stop feeding drama, it loses its power over you and the people who enjoy stirring conflict will eventually look elsewhere for their stage. Your energy belongs to better things.

23. Cheer louder for your besties

Friendship is not meant to be a scoreboard. When your closest friends succeed, treat their victories as if they were your own. Celebrate promotions, cheer for creative projects, share their wins proudly. The more you lift them, the more your bond strengthens, because joy multiplies when shared. Supporting your friends also rewires your perspective. It teaches you to see their growth not as competition but as evidence that success is possible for all of you. When your circle rises together, everyone climbs higher than they could alone. This habit makes friendships deeper, more resilient and free of hidden resentment. Over time, you learn to see love and loyalty as the real markers of success, not who reaches milestones first.

24. Compete only with yourself

The only competition that makes sense is the one with yesterday's version of you. When you compare yourself to others, you chase goals that were never meant for you. But when you measure against your own progress, every step forward counts. Maybe today you handled stress better than last week. Maybe you spoke up in a meeting where you once stayed silent. Maybe you simply got out of bed on a tough morning. Those are wins, even if no one else notices. Shifting the competition inward changes the game entirely. Instead of jealousy, you find motivation. Instead of exhaustion, you feel proud of progress that is real and personal. Every day offers a chance to outgrow the version of you that came before. That is the only scoreboard worth checking. And when you keep your focus there, life feels less like a race you can't win.

Cozy Nights Over Drama Nights

Cozy Nights Over Drama Nights:
Choosing comfort instead of chaos

Not every invitation deserves your energy, yet many women still push themselves into loud gatherings, late-night events or chaotic circles because they are afraid of missing out or of being judged if they decline. The result is often the same: you come home drained, overstimulated and wondering why you said yes in the first place. Society celebrates the busy, the social, the endlessly available, while rest is seen as laziness. But in truth, comfort is not a weakness, it is a choice that protects your peace. A quiet evening with tea, a blanket and a favorite book or series often nourishes far more than hours of small talk in a crowded room. Choosing coziness over chaos does not mean isolating yourself, it means curating your time with care. The more you honor what you truly need instead of following pressure, the more life feels like it belongs to you. A single cozy night can recharge you more than three chaotic ones combined. The art lies in realizing that saying no to drama is saying yes to balance and that balance is what allows you to thrive.

"There is nothing like staying at home for real comfort."
– Jane Austen

25. Learn to love your own company

Spending an evening alone does not have to feel empty. A cozy night at home is not the absence of people, it is the presence of yourself. The trick is to plan it with the same care you would if a friend were visiting. Cook your favorite meal, light a candle or play music that fits your mood. At first you may feel restless, tempted to scroll or wonder what others are doing, but if you stay with it, you will discover the calm of being on your own terms. Solitude is not a punishment, it is a space where you can hear yourself think and feel without interruption. When you start treating your own company as valuable, you stop running from it. These nights strengthen independence and make social time richer, because you no longer go out to escape yourself but because you genuinely want to.

26. Redefine what fun means

Fun is not a universal formula, though many people pretend it is. For some, fun is dancing until sunrise, for others it is reading thrillers in bed or baking cookies on a rainy night. When you accept that fun is personal, you free yourself from outside pressure. Start by asking which activities make you lose track of time in the best way. Then allow yourself to call that fun, even if it does not look exciting on social media. When you stop borrowing other people's idea of joy, you finally start living by your own. Redefining fun this way stops you from forcing yourself into nights that leave you drained. Instead, you fill your life with experiences that genuinely restore you and reflect who you are.

27. Protect your evenings like sacred time

Evenings are the natural reset button of the day, yet they vanish quickly when you give them away without thought. If you agree to every invitation, every extra task or every last-minute request, you end up drained before the new day begins. Protecting your evenings means deciding in advance how you want to spend them and guarding that choice with intention. Maybe you reserve two nights a week for friends and keep the others for yourself. Maybe you commit to small rituals like tea, stretching or journaling. These cues tell your body it is safe to slow down. When you treat evenings as sacred, you stop giving away your best hours to things that do not serve you. Soon, nights once called boring become the anchor that holds your balance.

28. Choose relationships that feel like home

The company you keep at night matters as much as what you do. Even the coziest setting turns heavy if it is shared with people who thrive on conflict and chaos. Pay attention to how you feel after spending time with someone. Do you leave lighter or more tense? Do you feel seen or criticized? Relationships that feel like home create safety and warmth, allowing even a simple meal or quiet chat to restore your energy. Peaceful company is often more exciting than the loudest party. Surround yourself with people who value comfort, kindness and calm. With them, cozy nights transform into true connection instead of wasted hours. Over time, these bonds become the foundation of a more stable and joyful life.

Laugh More, Stress Less

Laugh More, Stress Less:
How humor keeps you young

Life is full of situations that could either break you or make you laugh and the choice often decides how heavy or how light the moment feels. Stress is unavoidable, but the way you respond to it shapes your entire experience. When you choose humor, even in small doses, you create a buffer between yourself and the pressure of the world. A silly joke, a playful perspective or a burst of laughter with a friend can dissolve tension faster than any lecture on calmness. Yet most adults forget how to laugh freely. They associate humor with childishness, as if growing older means replacing joy with solemnity. In truth, the opposite is required: the more responsibilities you carry, the more you need humor to keep from collapsing under the weight. Laughter lowers stress hormones, relaxes muscles and connects you instantly with others. One shared laugh can turn a stranger into a friend or a hard day into a bearable one. Choosing humor does not mean ignoring problems, it means facing them with resilience and reminding yourself that you are bigger than the stress trying to consume you.

"Laughter is timeless.
Imagination has no age. And
dreams are forever."
– Walt Disney

29. Watch comedy on purpose

Laughter should not be an accident, it should be a practice. Make comedy part of your routine by choosing shows, podcasts or stand-up specials that reliably make you smile. When you deliberately reach for humor, you interrupt spirals of stress before they take root. Scientists have shown that laughter lowers cortisol, boosts immunity and even improves circulation. More importantly, it lightens your spirit in ways that words of advice rarely can. Think of comedy as daily exercise for your mood. A few minutes of laughter can flip the switch on a heavy day, helping you return to problems with fresh energy. When you treat humor like medicine, you remember that joy is not a luxury but a resource you can refill whenever you choose.

30. Laugh at your own mistakes

Everyone trips, forgets or spills something at some point, but not everyone knows how to recover with grace. The habit of laughing at your errors is more powerful than you think. Instead of turning every mishap into proof of failure, you transform it into a story. Humor cuts the shame in half and frees you to move forward. Think of the last time you stumbled and others laughed with you, not at you. It probably bonded you more than a flawless performance ever could. Treat small accidents as material for comedy and they lose their sting. Laughter turns mistakes into reminders that you are human, not into weights that keep you stuck. With time, you discover that self-irony is one of the strongest shields against bitterness.

31. Share silly moments with friends
Stress shrinks when it is laughed at together. Think about the times you and a friend could not stop giggling over something ridiculous. Those moments stay with you longer than the serious ones. Shared laughter deepens bonds, because it signals safety and trust. It says: here we can drop the mask, here we can be real. Make space for these silly moments by not always steering conversations toward problems or achievements. Watch a funny video together, share a childhood memory that still makes you laugh or simply let yourself be playful without fear of looking foolish. When you create room for laughter in friendships, you strengthen them more than any heavy discussion ever could. Over time, you will find that these shared moments become the glue that holds relationships steady, even during harder days.

32. Collect funny memories
Humor fades quickly if you do not save it, but when you collect funny memories, you create a personal archive of joy. Write down inside jokes, save screenshots of hilarious texts or keep a notebook of moments that made you laugh until your stomach hurt. On difficult days, flipping through this collection works like medicine. It reminds you that life is not only heavy, that there have been countless moments of lightness already and more will come. By keeping these memories close, you give yourself tools to fight stress when it feels overwhelming. Over the years, this archive becomes a map of your happiest moments and a resource you can revisit whenever you need to lift your spirit.

Move Your Body, Lift Your Mood

Move Your Body, Lift Your Mood:
Why motion is the best medicine

Your body was never designed to sit for hours, staring at glowing screens while your shoulders tighten and your breath grows shallow. Yet modern life demands it and many people treat stillness as the default. The cost shows up quietly: tension in the back, restless sleep, low energy, a mood that sinks without clear reason. Movement is the antidote. Each time you move, you tell your nervous system that you are alive and safe. Science shows that even ten minutes of movement can lift endorphins, those natural mood-boosters that work faster than most pep talks. Too often, people treat exercise as punishment for eating or as a desperate attempt to change appearance. But motion should not be tied to guilt. It is a gift to yourself. The more you view it as nourishment rather than obligation, the easier it becomes to weave into daily life. Over time, movement turns into a habit that carries you through stress, keeps you grounded and reminds you that joy lives as much in the body as in the mind.

"Those who think they have not time for bodily exercise will sooner or later have to find time for illness."
– Edward Stanley

33. Take walking breaks during the day

Sitting for long hours drains energy more than heavy tasks ever could. A short walk interrupts that spiral instantly. Step outside for ten minutes, circle your block or simply walk through the building while breathing deeply. As your body moves, your circulation wakes up, your posture resets and your mind unclutters. Walking is underestimated because it looks too easy, yet it is one of the most effective ways to recharge. Do it once and you feel a lift, do it daily and it becomes a quiet anchor in your routine. The true magic of walking is not only in moving your body, but in reminding your brain that you are not stuck. Each step forward is proof that you can create change, even on days that feel heavy. And that sense of momentum spills into everything else you do.

34. Dance in your living room

Movement does not need to be serious to be effective. Dancing, even alone in your kitchen, floods your body with endorphins and makes stress slide off your shoulders. Put on music that makes you smile and let yourself move however you want. No choreography, no judgment. Just freedom. Five minutes of dancing can change your mood faster than an hour of scrolling ever could. It reconnects you with the playful energy most adults forget they still have. When you dance, you remind yourself that joy belongs in the body, not just in the mind. What starts as a small act of silliness quickly becomes one of the most powerful tools for lifting energy. And the best part: you never need equipment, training or approval. Just press play and let go.

35. Turn chores into mini workouts

Housework often feels like a burden, but with the right mindset it can double as a workout. Carrying laundry becomes strength training, vacuuming turns into cardio and scrubbing the floor works muscles you forgot you had. Instead of rushing through chores mindlessly, add intention: squat while picking things up, lunge while moving around or put on upbeat music and match your pace to the rhythm. Suddenly, tasks that once felt draining become a source of energy. When you turn chores into movement, you reclaim time you thought was wasted. By the end, your home looks better, your body feels looser and your mind is lighter. It is proof that you do not need a gym or perfect schedule to stay active. You only need creativity and the decision to see every task as an opportunity to move.

36. Get fresh air daily

Movement feels different outdoors. Even a short walk outside shifts your mood more than the same steps indoors. The combination of fresh air, changing scenery and natural light resets both body and mind. Make it a rule to step outside at least once a day, whether for a stroll during lunch, a walk to run errands or simply standing on a balcony with deep breaths. Your nervous system calms when it connects with the environment beyond walls and screens. Over time, this habit improves sleep, reduces stress and makes daily life feel less boxed in. It is one of the simplest practices with the greatest return and it never requires more than the willingness to open the door.

Master Your Evening Routine

Master Your Evening Routine:
How calm nights create balance

The way you end your day shapes how you feel, think and recover. Many people treat evenings as leftover hours, filling them with random tasks, scrolling or half-watching shows while the mind still races. By the time they fall into bed, their body is restless and their thoughts refuse to settle. A clear evening routine changes that. It is not about strict schedules or perfection, it is about creating a gentle structure that tells your body and mind: the day is done, now it is safe to let go. Rituals do not need to be complicated. They can be as simple as dimming the lights, making a cup of tea or writing down tomorrow's to-do list so your brain can finally relax. The purpose of an evening routine is not to add more work but to subtract the noise that keeps you awake. When evenings become intentional, they turn into anchors of peace. They prepare you not only for better sleep but for better days, because you start from a place of calm instead of chaos. The more you practice this, the more you realize that rest is not something you collapse into. It is something you create with care.

"Sleep is the best meditation."
– Dalai Lama

37. Release the day, don't carry it

Evenings are not meant for rehearsing tomorrow, they are for letting go of today. Before you head to bed, spend ten minutes clearing your mental desk. Write down the worries, tasks or random thoughts that would otherwise follow you under the covers. Put them on paper so your brain no longer has to juggle them. Pair this with a small act of release: close the laptop, tidy one corner or take a slow breath at the window. These cues tell your body the workday is finished and nothing urgent remains. Instead of falling asleep with a storm of "shoulds" circling your head, you give yourself the gift of closure. The day can end peacefully because you decided it does.

38. Dim the digital noise

Screens trick your brain into believing it is still daytime. Blue light delays melatonin and endless scrolling keeps your mind racing long after you want to rest. Creating a "digital sunset" is one of the most effective evening habits. Decide on a time when devices go away, even if it is just 30 minutes before bed. Replace the noise with rituals that signal peace: a warm shower, light stretching or reading something enjoyable. These swaps calm your nervous system and prepare you for deep rest. By dimming digital noise, you protect your sleep and reclaim evenings as a space of quiet, not distraction. You will soon find that your dreams become deeper and your mornings easier, because your brain has had the chance to reset. Even your eyes will thank you, since screen breaks reduce strain and headaches. This small change can grow into one of the most powerful routines for long-term health and balance.

39. End the day with self-care

Evenings are not just the leftovers of a long day, they are a chance to take back control and remind yourself that you are more than what you accomplished in the past twelve hours. Too often, nights get swallowed by exhaustion and you tumble into bed carrying stress that should have been left behind. The simplest way to undo the day's chaos is to care for yourself. It does not have to be fancy or expensive, it simply has to be intentional. When you slow down at night and treat yourself kindly, you are sending a message to your body and mind that you matter. Think of it as closing the book on the day with a gentle ritual. Slip into clothes that feel good against your skin, wash your face slowly instead of rushing through the motions or take a shower that feels more like a reset than a chore. Brew a cup of tea, light a candle or simply pause for a moment of quiet before bed. You can romanticize the moment by adding soft music or a favorite scent, turning a simple ritual into something calming and almost ceremonial. Even brushing your hair slowly or applying hand cream with care can become signals that the day is done. Self-care at night is about creating an atmosphere that soothes, reassures and reminds you that you deserve ease.

With consistency, these choices build resilience. You begin to fall asleep not with leftover tension, but with a sense of calm. Your body repairs better, your mind processes more clearly and your spirit learns that rest is not wasted time but a form of strength. You choose to end the day on your own terms, with rituals that protect your energy and preserve your joy.

Declutter Your Space, Declutter Your Mind

Declutter Your Space, Declutter Your Mind: Why order brings peace

Your environment shapes your mood more than you think. A messy desk, piles of laundry or drawers stuffed with things you never use all create background stress. Your brain sees each item as unfinished business, which quietly drains your focus and energy. In contrast, a clear space signals calm. It tells you that things are under control and allows your mind to settle. Decluttering is not about perfection, it is about creating an atmosphere that supports peace. You do not need to live like a minimalist or throw away half your belongings. Start small: clear one shelf, tidy a corner or donate a few items you no longer need. Each small step makes you feel lighter, because you are letting go of both physical and mental clutter. Over time, your home begins to feel less like a storage unit and more like a sanctuary where you can breathe and recharge. Order outside creates space inside and that is often enough to change how you experience daily life.

"Have nothing in your houses that you do not know to be useful or believe to be beautiful."
– William Morris

40. Start small with one space

Decluttering feels overwhelming if you try to handle your entire home at once. The secret is to focus on a single area, like a drawer, a desk corner or one shelf. When you finish even a small space, the sense of progress motivates you to keep going. A tiny win shows you that change is possible and momentum grows from there. Break large areas into manageable sections and treat each one as a finished project. This way you avoid the exhaustion of taking on too much at once. Instead of postponing because it feels impossible, you prove to yourself that it can be done. Over time, those little clearings accumulate and suddenly entire rooms feel lighter. The result is not just a cleaner home but a calmer mind, because you no longer live surrounded by unfinished business.

41. Follow the one-in, one-out rule

Clutter creeps back when new things arrive but nothing leaves. To stop this cycle, adopt the one-in, one-out rule. Every time you bring home something new, remove one similar item you no longer use. This simple balance keeps order and prevents your home from slowly filling up again. It also makes you more intentional about what you buy, because you weigh carefully whether the new item is worth replacing something you already own. The rule sounds small, but its long-term impact is huge. It stops clutter before it starts, sparing you the stress of another big clean-up. By practicing it consistently, you maintain the peace you worked so hard to create. A home with steady balance feels light, easy to navigate, and more welcoming, not just for others but for yourself as well.

42. Donate instead of storing

Many people hold on to things they never use because they feel guilty throwing them away. But objects that sit in closets or basements do not serve you. By donating, you transform clutter into something meaningful. Clothes, books or kitchen tools you ignore could be valuable for someone else. The act of giving creates lightness twice: your space becomes freer and someone else gains something useful. Start with a simple rule: if you have not touched it in a year, you probably do not need it. Instead of letting belongings gather dust, release them to a new home where they can be appreciated. Decluttering then becomes more than tidying, it becomes an act of kindness. The more often you practice it, the easier it is to let go, because you see how positive the effect can be.

43. Keep surfaces clear

Clutter multiplies fastest on flat spaces. Tables, countertops and desks attract objects until they disappear under piles. Make it a habit to leave surfaces clear at the end of each day. When you walk into a room and see open space, your mind feels instantly calmer. Clear surfaces act like a reset button, telling your brain that the environment is under control. Put things back in drawers or baskets instead of dropping them on the nearest flat spot. Once you get used to the habit, you will notice how much more welcoming your home feels. Even five minutes in the evening can be enough to restore order. When you protect your space from clutter, you protect your focus, your mood and your ability to relax without distraction.

Money as Freedom, Not Stress

Money as Freedom, Not Stress:
Change how you see finances

Money often feels like a constant source of worry. Bills, unexpected costs or comparing yourself to others can turn it into a weight that never leaves your shoulders. Yet money itself is not the enemy, it is the way we think about it. When you treat money only as a measure of status, it will always create pressure. When you see it as a tool, it becomes a form of freedom. Financial calm does not come from chasing endless amounts, it comes from knowing what you need and creating habits that support it. Small steps like tracking spending, saving for goals or cutting unnecessary costs build confidence. Each conscious decision turns money from a stressor into an ally. The goal is not to restrict yourself harshly but to make money serve your values instead of your fears. When your finances align with what matters most, you feel lighter, safer and more in control of your future.

"Do not save what is left after spending, but spend what is left after saving."
- Warren Buffett

44. Track your spending without judgment

Most people avoid looking at their numbers because they fear what they will find. But ignoring expenses only makes anxiety grow. Start by tracking where your money goes each week, not to punish yourself but to gain clarity. Write it down in a notebook, use an app or check statements regularly. Once you see the truth, you realize it is less scary than the unknown. Awareness is the first step toward control. Maybe you spend more on takeout than you thought or subscriptions you forgot about are draining cash. With this knowledge, you can make small changes that add up. The key is to treat tracking as neutral information, not as a judgment on your worth. Eventually, you begin to feel lighter, because money stops being a vague worry and becomes something you actively understand and manage.

45. Build a safety cushion

Stress about money often comes from fear of emergencies. A broken phone or a sudden bill can feel overwhelming if you have no backup. Creating an emergency fund, even if small, changes that instantly. Aim for one month of expenses first, then build slowly. With money set aside, unexpected events stop being crises and turn into solvable problems. You respond calmly instead of panicking, because you know you prepared. Saving can feel slow, but the security it brings is worth more than any impulse purchase. Over time, the habit of putting aside a little adds up to real freedom, because you no longer live at the edge of stress with every small surprise life throws at you.

46. Spend on what brings value

Cutting costs does not mean stripping life of joy. It means choosing consciously. Many people waste money on things they barely notice while denying themselves purchases that truly matter. Take time to ask: does this expense make my life better, easier or happier? If yes, it is worth keeping. If not, let it go. Buying a quality item that lasts or an experience that creates memories is far more valuable than chasing cheap thrills that fade instantly. By aligning spending with your values, you remove regret and make your financial decisions feel empowering. Each purchase becomes intentional, a reflection of what you stand for rather than an impulse to fill space. This approach replaces stress with satisfaction and turns money into a tool for joy.

47. Separate money from status

Much of financial stress comes from comparison. People chase cars, clothes or homes not because they need them but because they fear falling behind. The result is endless spending that never satisfies. Break the cycle by redefining what success means to you. If financial calm and freedom are your true goals, let go of the urge to prove worth with price tags. Wealth is not what people see, it is what protects you when no one is looking. Focus on savings, investments or simply stability and notice how much lighter you feel. The less you connect money to status, the more you can enjoy it as a resource that supports your life instead of controlling it. In the end, your bank balance matters less than whether your money aligns with your peace.

Nourish, Don't Punish

Nourish, Don't Punish:
Building a kinder relationship with food

Food is one of life's simplest joys, yet for many it becomes a battlefield. Diet culture has taught people to see eating as punishment, as if meals must be earned and guilt is the price of enjoyment. This mindset does not create health, it creates fear. Real balance comes from nourishment, not restriction. When you treat food as fuel and pleasure, you stop fighting with your body and start supporting it. Eating becomes less about counting and more about caring. Your body does not need perfection, it needs consistency and kindness. Nutritious meals can be colorful, flavorful and satisfying and they give you energy instead of shame. By shifting your focus from punishment to nourishment, you begin to trust yourself again. Food becomes less about rules and more about freedom, because it serves your well-being instead of your insecurity. That shift transforms not just how you eat, but how you feel about yourself.

"Let food be thy medicine and medicine be thy food."
– Hippocrates

48. Focus on adding, not restricting

Most diets start with lists of what you "cannot" eat, which makes food feel like punishment. Instead, shift your focus to what you can add: more colorful vegetables, fruits, grains or proteins that make you feel energized. By adding nourishing foods first, you naturally crowd out the less healthy ones without harsh rules. This creates a positive cycle. You feel better, so you want more of the foods that support you. When eating becomes about abundance instead of restriction, it feels like freedom, not control. You stop obsessing over cutting things out and begin celebrating what goes on your plate. This approach not only supports long-term health but also helps repair your relationship with food, because meals become moments of joy and care instead of guilt and fear.

49. Listen to your body's signals

Your body speaks constantly, but many people have learned to ignore it. Hunger cues, fullness signals or cravings are treated as enemies instead of information. Reconnecting with these signals helps you eat in ways that truly satisfy. Pause before meals and ask: am I physically hungry or am I stressed, bored or tired? During eating, notice when your body feels content instead of stuffed. Trusting your signals builds confidence that your body knows what it needs. This practice turns meals into a dialogue rather than a battle. It takes time, but with consistency you begin to recognize patterns and respond with care instead of judgment. Food stops being about external rules and becomes about internal wisdom, which is the most sustainable guide you can follow.

50. Eat without distraction

Modern life encourages multitasking, even at the table. People eat while scrolling, working or watching TV and then wonder why meals feel unsatisfying. When your attention is elsewhere, your brain barely registers what you consumed. Slow down and give meals your full focus. Notice flavors, textures and how your body feels as you eat. This simple practice improves digestion, reduces overeating and helps you enjoy food more. Mindful eating transforms ordinary meals into moments of calm. Even one phone-free meal a day can reset your relationship with food. Over time, you discover that eating without distraction is not only healthier but also more joyful, because meals become an experience instead of another task rushed through without thought.

51. Ditch the guilt around treats

Enjoying dessert or a favorite snack does not erase healthy choices. Food is not a moral test, it is nourishment and pleasure. Allowing treats without guilt makes your diet sustainable, because restriction usually leads to rebellion. Balance comes from flexibility, not perfection. By giving yourself permission to indulge occasionally, you remove the cycle of shame and bingeing. A healthy mindset includes joy as well as discipline. One slice of cake does not define your health, just as one salad does not either. What matters is the pattern over time. When you stop attaching guilt to food, you free yourself to eat with more confidence, less stress and more trust in your ability to find balance naturally.

Beauty Without Pressure

Beauty Without Pressure:
Redefining what it means to look good

Beauty should be a source of joy, not a source of stress. Yet many people treat it like a competition, measuring themselves against impossible standards set by ads, filters or social media. The result is constant pressure: every wrinkle feels like failure, every bad hair day like proof you are not enough. But true beauty does not come from chasing perfection, it comes from authenticity. Confidence, warmth and presence shine brighter than flawless skin ever could. When beauty is rooted in self-respect, it becomes sustainable. Taking care of yourself should feel like a gift, not an obligation. This means choosing routines that make you feel good, whether that is skincare, style or rest, without comparing yourself to anyone else. By releasing pressure, beauty turns into self-expression instead of self-criticism. Over time, you realize that the most attractive quality is not how you look but how at ease you are in your own skin.

"Beauty begins the moment you decide to be yourself."
– Coco Chanel

52. Care for your skin with kindness

Skincare should not be punishment for aging or flaws, but a way to nurture yourself. A simple routine (cleansing, moisturizing, protecting) does more than improve appearance, it creates a daily ritual of self-respect. Think of it as feeding your skin the same way you feed your body. Overcomplicating with endless products often leads to stress and waste. Focus on consistency and quality over hype. Your skin reflects care more than perfection. When you treat skincare as kindness instead of correction, the process feels grounding. Each time you care for your skin, you remind yourself that you deserve softness, rest and attention. Gradually, this mindset matters more than any single product, because confidence grows when care is rooted in self-love.

53. Choose style that feels like you

Fashion is too often treated as a race to keep up with trends, but style is about expression, not competition. Wear colors, cuts and textures that make you feel comfortable and confident. When clothes reflect your personality, they lift your energy instead of draining it. Stop chasing what others label as "must-haves" and build a wardrobe that supports your lifestyle. True style begins when you stop dressing to impress and start dressing to express. Choosing clothes that align with your values saves time and reduces stress, because you no longer feel pressured to fit in. Over time, your style becomes a quiet statement: not about status, but about confidence in who you are.

54. Redefine beauty standards for yourself

The world constantly changes its mind about what is beautiful. In one decade, curves are praised, in another, thinness is demanded. One era favors pale skin, another favors tanning. If you keep chasing these shifting rules, you will always feel behind. Instead, decide what beauty means for you and choose habits that support that definition. Look at history and culture as proof that the rules are negotiable. Start by noticing what makes you feel radiant: maybe it is rested skin, maybe it is wearing colors that brighten your mood or maybe it is simply feeling comfortable in your body. Remove triggers that fuel comparison (like certain social media accounts) and surround yourself with influences that value authenticity. Over time, that inner certainty makes you more magnetic than any fleeting trend ever could.

55. Rest as part of your beauty routine

The glow people chase in jars often comes from something much simpler: real rest. While makeup can cover fatigue, nothing replaces the quiet repair your body performs when you pause. Skin renews itself more effectively when stress levels drop, fine lines soften when muscles are not clenched all day and your natural expression changes when you are not running on empty. Instead of thinking of rest only as sleep, weave recovery into your days in small doses. Step away from the mirror for a moment, close your eyes and breathe deeply. Lie down for ten minutes without scrolling. By giving yourself time to recover, every product you use works better and your natural glow becomes harder to miss.

Friendships That Lift You Up

Friendships That Lift You Up:
Choosing people who make you stronger

The people around you quietly shape who you become. A friend's words, energy and habits rub off on you, whether you notice it or not. When friendships are heavy, filled with drama, criticism or constant competition, they drain more than they give. The opposite is true for uplifting friendships: they create a sense of safety, spark joy and remind you of your worth. These are the relationships that make you laugh until your stomach hurts, that listen without judgment and that celebrate your wins without envy. The right friendships act like mirrors that show your best self back to you. Choosing such connections requires intention. It means being honest about which relationships leave you feeling stronger and which leave you feeling small. It also means being brave enough to step back from people who drain you, even if history ties you together. Friendships are not about quantity, they are about quality. A few people who truly lift you up can change the tone of your entire life. When you protect your circle, you protect your energy and with that energy you are free to grow into the best version of yourself.

"Friendship is born at that moment when one person says to another, 'What! You too? I thought I was the only one.'"
– C. S. Lewis

56. Notice how you feel after spending time together

The best way to judge a friendship is not by history or promises but by how you feel once you part ways. Do you walk away lighter, more confident and energized or do you feel small, drained or unsettled? Your body often tells the truth before your mind does. Start paying attention to these signals. Keep a mental note after each interaction and patterns will soon appear. Good friends leave you with warmth, not exhaustion. If a person consistently pulls you down, no amount of excuses can change that effect. It does not mean they are bad, but it does mean they are not right for your circle. By respecting your own feelings, you protect your energy and open space for people who bring out the best in you.

57. Create small rituals together

Strong friendships are not built only on big celebrations or dramatic stories, but on the tiny, repeated moments that weave your lives together. A weekly coffee, a Friday night call or even sending each other the same silly meme can become anchors in the relationship. These rituals are not about what you do, but about the consistency that reminds you: I am here and you are here too. Shared rituals give comfort because they turn friendship into something steady in a world that often feels rushed and unstable. They create little islands of belonging where you do not have to explain yourself or perform. These small traditions gradually turn into inside jokes and shared memories that no one else could invent for you. What seems ordinary at first slowly becomes the unique glue of your friendship.

58. Be the kind of friend you want to have

Strong friendships grow through reciprocity. If you want honesty, start by speaking truthfully. If you want loyalty, show up when it matters. Do not wait for others to make the first move, take the lead by modeling the qualities you admire. Call when you promise, answer messages even when life is busy and respect the boundaries your friends set. Small, steady actions build more trust than rare grand gestures. Consistency creates a sense of safety that people deeply value. Being supportive does not mean ignoring your own needs, it means balancing care for others with care for yourself. Over time, the way you show up attracts people who live by the same principles. The result is a circle of friends who reflect back the same kindness and integrity you bring into the relationship.

59. Let go when the bond no longer serves you

Not every friendship is designed to last forever. People change, priorities shift and sometimes paths naturally separate. Notice the signs: conversations feel heavy, trust fades or you leave interactions more tired than fulfilled. Accepting this does not erase past joy, it simply acknowledges reality. Letting go makes space for healthier connections to grow. It is painful at first, because endings often carry guilt, but freedom follows quickly. By stepping back, you allow yourself to find people who match who you are now, not who you were years ago. Ending respectfully honors both sides, because forced closeness is not real closeness. Friendships, like seasons, have cycles and releasing what no longer works is a form of wisdom, not failure.

Learn Something New Every Month

Learn Something New Every Month:
Keep curiosity alive

Life feels dull when every day looks the same. Routine can be comforting, but it can also shrink your world if nothing fresh enters it. One of the simplest ways to stay mentally alive is to commit to learning something new every month. This does not have to mean going back to school or mastering a complex subject. It can be as simple as trying a new recipe, picking up a hobby or reading a book outside your usual interests. The point is not mastery, the point is curiosity. Each time you stretch yourself, you build confidence. You remind your brain that it is capable of adapting, that growth is always possible. Even small skills add up and create a sense of momentum. Learning also adds joy, because novelty sparks energy. Think of how alive you feel when you understand something you never knew before. That spark is available whenever you choose to invite it. By treating learning as a regular practice instead of a rare event, you build a life that feels rich and open. Knowledge becomes less about pressure and more about play and that shift keeps you both grounded and growing.

"Live as if you were to die tomorrow. Learn as if you were to live forever."
- Mahatma Gandhi

60. Start with small, playful skills

Learning does not always mean heavy textbooks or endless hours of study. Begin with something light, like cooking a new dish, learning a few words in another language or trying a simple craft. Small skills are easier to start and finishing them quickly gives you a sense of progress. Progress fuels motivation, because the brain loves completion. The more you finish, the more you want to continue. Tiny steps keep curiosity alive. Treat each new skill as an experiment, not a lifelong commitment. If you enjoy it, continue. If not, move on without guilt. Over time, these playful experiments create a wide collection of knowledge that makes life more interesting. Even skills you never master add color and stories to your days.

61. Schedule learning like an appointment

Good intentions fade if you never make time for them. Learning needs space in your calendar, just like exercise or rest. Choose one hour a week and treat it as a non-negotiable date with yourself. Use that time to watch tutorials, practice a hobby or read something new. When you schedule it, you stop waiting for "free time" that never comes. The regularity matters more than the length, because small, repeated effort grows into lasting change. Discipline protects curiosity from being buried under daily tasks. It also takes away the pressure to be perfect, because you know another session is already waiting. Over weeks, you will notice progress you would never achieve if you relied on motivation alone. By respecting learning as important, you send yourself the message that growth is worth your time.

62. Learn from people, not only from books

Knowledge does not live only in libraries or online courses. Some of the most valuable lessons come from conversations. Ask a friend to show you their hobby or listen to a colleague explain a skill you never tried. Curiosity builds bridges between people. When you ask questions, you also give others the chance to shine by sharing what they know. The exchange becomes more than information, it becomes connection. Even brief encounters can leave lasting ideas. Chatting with a barista about coffee beans or asking a gardener about plants, can open doors you never expected. Learning from people adds color and context that books cannot always give. It reminds you that wisdom is everywhere if you stay open. These small exchanges create a web of insight that makes the world feel bigger and friendlier.

63. Keep a curiosity journal

New experiences fade quickly if you do not capture them. A curiosity journal helps you track what you learn and reflect on how it changes you. Write down what you tried, how it felt and what surprised you. This turns vague memories into concrete lessons. Looking back, you see proof of your growth month by month. The journal also helps you choose what to explore next, because patterns emerge. Maybe you realize you enjoy creative activities more than technical ones or that languages energize you more than cooking. The more you write, the easier it is to notice progress and progress fuels motivation. Soon the journal becomes a treasure chest of experiences that remind you how much you are capable of learning.

Adventure Keeps You Young

Adventure Keeps You Young:
Say Yes to the Unexpected

Learning something new keeps the mind alive, but adventure takes the idea further. It puts curiosity into action. You do not need to climb mountains or run marathons to feel its effect. Adventure begins the moment you choose something unexpected: taking a path you have never walked, saying yes to an invitation that feels unusual or daring to try something that makes your heart race a little faster. These moments spark a kind of energy that no book or class can replace. The beauty of adventure is that it pulls you out of autopilot and gives you stories to tell. Children look at the world expecting surprises, which is why everything feels like play. Adults forget that sense of wonder and with it, some of their vitality. By welcoming adventure back into your life, you remind yourself that discovery is not just for the young. It is not about risk or extremes, but about keeping your days alive with possibility. And that mindset will keep you glowing from the inside out.

"Life is either a daring adventure or nothing at all."
- Helen Keller

64. Say yes to small risks

Adventure often begins in the space where comfort ends. Choose one thing each week that feels a little uncertain and say yes to it. Order the dish you have never tried, take a new path home, speak first in a group or join an activity that makes your heart race slightly. Keep the stakes low and the mood playful. Small risks teach your mind and body that the unknown is not dangerous, only different. They sharpen awareness, boost energy and remind you that flexibility is a strength. Create a simple rule for yourself: when the choice is between the usual and the slightly daring, lean toward the second. Write these moments down to see how they add up. This mindset slowly shifts your life from predictable to surprising and those surprises are what keep you feeling young.

65. Explore places close to home

Adventure does not always require a plane ticket. A sense of wonder can thrive in your own city if you choose to see it with new eyes. Visit a museum you have never entered, try a restaurant outside your usual habits or spend an afternoon in a neighborhood you rarely pass through. These small acts of exploration refresh your perspective. They remind you that novelty is everywhere, not just far away. By treating your local world as something worth discovering, you train yourself to notice beauty in the everyday. This habit builds appreciation for where you live and keeps life from feeling flat. When you collect these mini adventures, you create a map of joy close to home. The effect is the same as travel: excitement, newness and stories you can share, all without leaving your own city.

66. Do something a little ridiculous

Not every act of courage has to involve fear. Sometimes the bravest move is letting yourself look silly. Sing loudly even if you miss half the notes or dance in the street without caring if anyone is watching. These moments are small rebellions against the pressure to always look polished and composed. They remind you that joy does not depend on approval and that laughter at yourself can be one of the healthiest forms of confidence. The gift of being ridiculous is that it frees you from perfection. You stop measuring your value by how impressive you appear and instead embrace the lightness of simply being human. A silly moment can dissolve stress faster than hours of overthinking and it often turns into the story that everyone remembers.

67. Collect stories, not just achievements

Success is often measured by titles, possessions or numbers, but the richest parts of life are the stories you carry. Adventures remind you that imperfect moments are often the ones that stay with you. Getting lost on a trip, laughing through a failed recipe or meeting someone unexpected can turn into tales you tell for years. These memories give depth to your life in ways trophies or certificates never could. Focusing on stories shifts your perspective from outcome to experience. Instead of chasing perfection, you embrace the messiness of living fully. Your collection of memories becomes a reminder that your life was not just measured by what you achieved but by what you experienced and those experiences keep your spirit young.

Write It Down, Clear It Out

Write It Down, Clear It Out:
The power of journaling

Thoughts build up like clutter in a room. If they stay unspoken, they circle endlessly, leaving you restless and unfocused. Writing is one of the simplest ways to break that loop. Putting words on paper gives shape to what feels chaotic and once it has shape, it loses power. Journaling does not require talent or perfect sentences. It only requires honesty. You can write about frustrations, goals, memories or random ideas. The act itself is what creates clarity. A page absorbs what your mind no longer needs to carry. The more often you write, the lighter you feel. Problems shrink once they are seen and patterns become visible that you missed before. Over time, your journal becomes a mirror, showing you how far you have come. It is a private space that belongs only to you, free of judgment, where you can say what cannot be said out loud. A journal is both a record of your days and a release for your thoughts, giving you room to breathe.

"Journal writing is a voyage to the interior."
- Christina Baldwin

68. Use journaling to unload worries

When your mind feels crowded, writing turns invisible stress into visible words. Sit down with a notebook and write freely about what bothers you. Do not worry about grammar or structure. The goal is to move thoughts out of your head and onto the page. Once written, they lose intensity. You begin to see worries as problems that can be solved, not endless loops of anxiety. Writing is like clearing mental clutter, one line at a time. Try this before bed to quiet your thoughts or in the morning to start with a lighter mind. Even five minutes makes a difference. Over time, the pages become a safe container for emotions, frustrations and fears that would otherwise weigh you down. Instead of carrying them all day, you leave them on paper and walk away with more clarity and peace.

69. Track progress and patterns

A journal is not only for venting, it is also a tool for growth. By recording daily or weekly notes, you can see how your moods, habits or challenges change over time. Patterns become visible that you would not notice in the rush of daily life. Maybe stress always rises after too little sleep or energy improves when you walk more. These insights turn vague feelings into clear evidence. Writing makes invisible connections visible. Looking back helps you celebrate progress too, because you notice how much you have overcome or improved. Journaling turns your life into a map where trends, triggers and victories can be traced. These records guide you to smarter choices and remind you that you are capable of change. What felt stuck yesterday becomes growth you can measure today.

70. Write letters you never send

There are feelings that are too heavy to carry yet too complex to express face to face. A safe way to release them is to write letters you will never send. Address them to people who hurt you, to people you miss or even to yourself. The act of writing gives shape to emotions that otherwise remain tangled. Once they are on paper, they lose intensity and become easier to understand. You can say everything you need to say without fear of judgment, interruption or conflict. This practice often reveals hidden layers of emotion that talking out loud could never uncover. It gives you clarity, closure and often forgiveness, because the words no longer circle endlessly in your mind. Over time, writing these letters becomes a tool to lighten old burdens and create space for healing.

71. Use prompts when you feel stuck

Some days you want to write but your mind feels empty. This is where prompts can help. Prompts act like small keys that unlock deeper thoughts. They guide your pen into motion and break through the resistance of a blank page. Try simple questions such as: What gave me joy today, what drained my energy, what do I want to release? Each answer leads to reflections you may not expect. Prompts do not limit you, they give direction without pressure. Keep a list of your favorite ones ready, so you never have to wait for inspiration. Over time, this habit shows you patterns you would not notice otherwise. Even short responses build self-awareness and remind you that your journal is always a place of discovery.

Gratitude in Small Doses

Gratitude in Small Doses:
Noticing the little things

Gratitude is often seen as something grand, like writing long lists or keeping a perfect journal, but its real power lies in the small moments. When you pause to notice what you already have, your mind shifts away from what is missing. Gratitude is not denial of problems. You acknowledge the struggles while also making space for the good. Even tiny practices, like appreciating a meal, a kind word or a quiet moment, can change the tone of your day. Gratitude works best in small, regular doses that re-train your attention. The more you practice, the more natural it becomes. At first you might force yourself to find one thing a day, but soon you start noticing positives everywhere. A warm cup of coffee, the comfort of your bed, a laugh with a friend. Ordinary details become extraordinary when you let them. Gratitude does not erase challenges, but it keeps them from taking over. It reminds you that even in difficult seasons, beauty exists. Over time, this mindset builds resilience, because you train yourself to keep perspective.

"Gratitude turns what we have into enough."
– Aesop

72. Start with one daily note

Gratitude does not have to be complicated. Each day, write down one thing you are thankful for. It can be as simple as good weather, a funny message or the taste of your favorite meal. When you capture even the smallest moments, you train your brain to notice positives instead of rushing past them. The more often you practice, the easier it becomes to find something new. One note a day is enough to shift your mindset. Keep a small notebook by your bed or use the notes app on your phone. Over time, the collection grows into a reminder that your life is filled with more good than you sometimes realize. When you reread the notes, you relive those small joys, which strengthens the habit even more.

73. Share your gratitude with others

Gratitude grows stronger when it is spoken. Telling someone that you appreciate them not only uplifts you, it strengthens the bond you share. It could be thanking a friend for listening, telling a colleague their effort mattered or texting a family member that you value them. These words turn private gratitude into connection. Expressing thanks spreads positivity far beyond yourself. The act of recognition makes others feel seen and that often inspires them to pass it on. What starts as a simple thank-you can create a chain of kindness that circles back to you. Over time, gratitude becomes not just a practice but a culture in your relationships. You notice how much lighter interactions feel when appreciation becomes a habit instead of an exception.

74. Use gratitude to reframe challenges

It is easy to be thankful when life feels smooth, but the true strength of gratitude shows up in difficult moments. Challenges test your patience, drain your energy and make it tempting to focus only on what is wrong. Gratitude does not erase hardship, but it changes how you hold it. By searching for even one small positive within a struggle, you give yourself perspective. Maybe you are stressed at work, but you can be grateful for a colleague who makes you laugh. Maybe you are dealing with loss, but you can find comfort in the people who support you. Gratitude in hard times is not pretending everything is fine, it is remembering that light still exists even in dark seasons.

When you reframe challenges through gratitude, the pressure shifts. Problems stop feeling like endless walls and start looking like obstacles with cracks where light comes through. Writing down these moments helps you recognize that struggle and strength can exist side by side. Your mind learns not to collapse under stress but to balance it with what remains good. This balance is what creates resilience. You no longer feel defined only by what hurts, you also feel supported by what still gives hope. Gratitude becomes a tool of survival, not just celebration. It reminds you that even when life feels unfair, you are not empty-handed. There is always something, however small, that keeps you moving forward. That recognition is enough to make hard times feel lighter and to remind you that growth is still possible.

Celebrate Yourself
Without Shame

Celebrate Yourself Without Shame:
Owning your wins

Many people downplay their achievements because they fear being judged as arrogant. They shrink their joy, make excuses or brush off compliments. The problem is that when you constantly minimize yourself, you teach your mind that your efforts are never enough. Celebrating yourself is not about showing off, it is about recognizing the value of your work and your growth. When you honor your wins, even the small ones, you fuel confidence. You also build motivation to continue, because your brain connects effort with reward. Learning to celebrate without shame means changing the way you respond to success. Instead of saying "It was nothing," try saying "Thank you, I worked hard for it." Share your milestones with people who support you, not with those who diminish you. This practice shifts the focus from fear of judgment to pride in progress. Gradually, it becomes a habit to pause, reflect and appreciate what you accomplished. By doing this, you create a life where joy is not hidden, but welcomed as proof of your growth.

"Don't downgrade your dream just to fit your reality. Upgrade your conviction to match your destiny."
– Stuart Scott

75. Keep a record of your wins

Progress disappears quickly from memory because the human brain is designed to focus more on problems than achievements. To balance this bias, keep a personal record of every win you achieve. Write them in a notebook, save screenshots of kind words or create a folder on your phone where you collect moments of success. Do not only include major milestones, but also small steps that show effort, such as finishing a workout, completing a task or choosing rest when you needed it. Looking at this record on difficult days reminds you that you are not standing still but moving forward. Over time, the collection proves your persistence and strength. It shows you evidence of progress even when you feel stuck. It also encourages you to set bigger goals, because you can clearly see how much you have already overcome.

76. Accept compliments with grace

Many people feel uncomfortable with praise and respond by downplaying their effort or making a joke. This habit might seem modest, but it damages your confidence and dismisses the appreciation offered to you. When someone recognizes your work, the best answer is simple: say "Thank you." Accepting a compliment is not arrogance, it is acknowledgment of your effort and the kindness of the other person. Start small by practicing in everyday situations. If someone notices your outfit, your cooking or your dedication at work, pause and accept the words without deflection. This habit sends a clear signal to your mind that your work matters. Soon it becomes natural to accept appreciation with ease.

77. Create your own rituals of celebration

Waiting for others to notice your progress can leave you disappointed. Instead, design small rituals to honor yourself. Treat yourself to a special coffee after finishing a project, take a quiet walk after reaching a goal or write down the moment in a journal so it does not fade. These private celebrations tell your mind that effort matters, even if no one else sees it. Rituals create meaning around your progress and reinforce your motivation. They do not need to be expensive or dramatic, only intentional. Each time you pause to celebrate, you build the habit of valuing yourself. Over months, these rituals become anchors that remind you of how capable you are. They also replace the pressure of outside approval with inner recognition, which is more sustainable and more empowering in the long run.

78. Stop comparing your journey

Comparison kills joy faster than failure. When you measure your progress against someone else's, you ignore your unique path. Their timeline is not yours and their victories do not erase your own. Instead of competing, practice focusing on your personal growth. Look back at where you started, not at where others are. Progress is best measured by your own steps, not by someone else's race. When you remind yourself of this truth, you free energy that used to fuel envy. That energy can be redirected into your own projects, where it creates real momentum. Over time, celebrating yourself becomes easier, because you no longer view your life through the distorted lens of comparison. You see your progress as enough and enough is powerful.

Kindness Without Expectation

Kindness Without Expectation:
Giving without keeping score

True kindness is not about recognition or reward. It is the quiet choice to make someone else's day lighter, even when no one notices. Many people hold back kindness because they fear being taken for granted or because they expect something in return. But when kindness is tied to outcome, it loses its purity. Real kindness is powerful precisely because it is free. A smile, a thoughtful message or a small act of help can ripple farther than you imagine. When you give without expectation, you create space for genuine connection. Kindness also changes you. The act itself releases tension, builds empathy and reminds you that you are part of something bigger. It shifts focus away from your own worries and shows you how much good can be created with small actions. The best part is that kindness multiplies. People who experience it often pass it on, creating a chain of goodwill that spreads beyond your reach. Practicing kindness regularly does not mean letting people walk over you. It means choosing to contribute positively without demanding a return. That choice is both liberating and deeply strengthening.

Remember there's no such thing as a small act of kindness. Every act creates a ripple with no logical end." – Scott Adams

79. Practice small, invisible acts

Kindness does not need an audience to count. In fact, the most powerful gestures are often the ones no one sees. Hold the door for a stranger, let someone go first in line or send an encouraging message without signing your name. These actions remind you that kindness is about intention, not attention. When you remove the need for recognition, you experience the pure joy of giving. Invisible kindness also helps quiet the ego, because it teaches you that your value is not tied to applause. Over time, practicing small acts daily rewires your perspective. You notice more opportunities to contribute and feel more connected to the world around you. The impact may be silent, but it is real and it shapes both the receiver and the giver.

80. Give without keeping score

Many people give while secretly expecting something in return. This turns kindness into a transaction and when the return does not come, resentment grows. To practice real generosity, let go of the scorecard. Offer help, time or a kind word simply because you choose to. Freedom comes when kindness is its own reward. By releasing expectations, you protect yourself from disappointment and allow relationships to flourish without pressure. Others feel safer with you, because they sense your actions are genuine. Over time, giving without keeping track shifts your mindset. You begin to see kindness not as sacrifice but as strength, a resource you can share without losing. The act itself becomes fulfilling and that makes you both lighter and more resilient.

81. Be kind to yourself first

Many people try to pour kindness into others while running on empty themselves. The problem is that constant giving without self-care eventually leads to exhaustion and resentment. Real kindness begins with how you treat yourself. Speak to yourself with the same compassion you offer to a friend. Rest when you need it, forgive mistakes and acknowledge your efforts instead of only noticing flaws. Self-kindness builds the foundation that makes generosity sustainable. When your own needs are met, you give freely instead of reluctantly. This shift changes the tone of every interaction. Acts of kindness flow naturally when they are not forced and others can feel the difference. Kindness toward yourself becomes a quiet strength, one that fuels your ability to support others without burning out.

82. Let kindness ripple forward

One act of kindness can create a chain reaction that reaches far beyond you. Hold the door for someone and they may smile at the next person. Offer encouragement and it might inspire them to support someone else. These ripples often spread invisibly, but they matter. By practicing kindness without expectation, you plant seeds in places you may never visit. This perspective helps you trust that your actions count, even when you do not witness the results. You begin to see the world differently: not as a place where only big acts matter, but as one where countless small ripples create real change. Each act is a reminder that you are part of something bigger than yourself and that awareness brings strength.

Let Go of Control

Let Go of Control:
Finding peace in acceptance

Trying to control everything seems smart at first, because planning brings order and order feels safe. Yet the more you tighten your grip, the more fragile you become when life shifts by a few degrees. Control promises certainty, but it often delivers tension, second guessing and a constant scan for threats. Letting go is not the same as giving up. It is a deliberate choice to focus on what is truly yours to influence and to release the rest. That shift does not make you passive, it makes you flexible. You act where action matters and you stop wasting energy on outcomes you cannot command. Acceptance is practical wisdom, because it gives you back the energy you spend on worry. With that energy you respond faster, think clearer and recover sooner when plans change. You build quiet confidence, the kind that does not collapse when the script goes off track. Peace grows not from perfect control, but from trust in your ability to meet reality as it is and still move forward.

"You must learn to let go. Release the stress. You were never in control anyway."
– Steve Maraboli

83. Focus on what you can influence

Worry multiplies when you spend energy on things you cannot change. The key is to separate what is in your hands from what is not. You cannot control the weather, other people's opinions or sudden events, but you can control how you respond. This shift sounds simple, yet it transforms stress into clarity. Write down the challenge you face and draw two columns: one for what you can act on, one for what lies outside your reach. Then direct your energy toward the first column only. Action on the controllable is always more powerful than worry about the uncontrollable. The practice is freeing, because you stop wasting strength on battles you cannot win. This habit builds resilience, since your focus stays on progress instead of fear.

84. Accept imperfection in plans

Plans are useful, but reality never follows them exactly. When you expect perfection, every small change feels like failure. The healthier approach is to plan lightly, then stay ready to adjust. Imagine your plan as a map rather than a rigid script: it gives direction, but detours are part of the journey. Imperfection is not a mistake, it is the natural rhythm of life. Each time you adapt, you prove to yourself that flexibility is strength. You stop seeing disruptions as disasters and start treating them as opportunities to learn. This mindset removes unnecessary pressure and makes the process easier. The result is more peace, more creativity and less stress, because you finally allow life to unfold instead of forcing it into narrow lines.

85. Practice surrender in small ways

Letting go does not start with life-changing events, it begins in ordinary situations where the stakes are low. Allow a friend to choose the restaurant, let the train be late without complaining or accept that a meeting runs longer than planned. These moments test your patience, but they also train your ability to release control. The point is not passivity but trust. When you stop clinging to every outcome, you notice that life continues smoothly even without your tight grip. Each time you relax into uncertainty, you prove to yourself that you are capable of handling imperfection. Over weeks and months, this becomes a habit. You begin to carry less tension, because you no longer expect everything to bend to your will. What once felt like disaster becomes a simple variation in the flow of life.

86. Trust your ability to adapt

The urge to control comes from fear that without it you will not cope. Yet your past proves otherwise. Think back to situations that did not go as planned: a project that shifted, a relationship that changed, a challenge you never expected. Even then, you found a way through. These memories are evidence of resilience. Trust does not grow from rigid plans but from knowing you can respond when life surprises you. Confidence shifts from external order to inner stability. This perspective makes you calmer, because you are no longer preparing for disaster, you are trusting in your capacity to navigate it. That trust creates freedom far greater than any illusion of control ever could.

Time in Nature

Time in Nature:
Finding calm outside

Modern life keeps you indoors, surrounded by screens, deadlines and noise. This constant pressure disconnects you from the rhythms of the natural world. Nature offers the opposite: quiet, space and perspective. Stepping outside, even for a short walk, resets your nervous system. The sound of leaves, the feel of fresh air and the sight of open sky bring balance that no device can give. Nature reminds you that life is larger than your current worries. Spending time outdoors does not require wilderness adventures. It can be as simple as sitting in a park, tending to plants on a balcony or pausing to watch the clouds. These moments provide more than relaxation, they sharpen awareness and restore focus. Studies show that nature lowers stress, improves mood and boosts creativity. The more often you reconnect, the more resilient you feel in daily life. Nature does not demand productivity, it simply invites presence. By making space for it regularly, you create a habit that grounds you, energizes you and gives you perspective no matter what challenges you face.

"In every walk with nature one receives far more than he seeks."
– John Muir

87. Take daily micro-adventures outside

You do not need a forest to feel the benefits of nature. Even short outdoor breaks can reset your body and mind. Step outside during lunch, walk a different route home or spend ten minutes on a bench in the park. These micro-adventures sound small, yet they create a powerful rhythm of pause and refresh. The key is consistency, not distance. Fresh air clears the head faster than scrolling a feed and changing your environment interrupts repetitive thought loops. These regular breaks build resilience. You feel less trapped in routine and more connected to the wider world. Each moment outside acts as a reset button, reminding you that life is not just tasks and screens but also wind, sky and open space.

88. Bring nature closer to your home

Not every day allows for long walks, but you can invite nature into your immediate space. Add plants to your living room, keep flowers on your desk or open the window to hear birds in the morning. These details seem minor, but they shift the atmosphere. Your environment becomes softer, fresher and more alive. Surrounding yourself with natural elements creates calm even when you cannot step outside. Research shows that indoor plants improve focus and reduce stress. Caring for them also builds a rhythm of nurture that grounds you. These small touches bring nature into your daily life in ways that feel effortless. The more you blend indoors with outdoors, the more you create a balanced space that supports rest, clarity and creativity without requiring extra time.

89. Use nature to reset perspective

Stress often makes your world feel small. Problems grow larger when they are all you can see. Stepping into nature shifts that perspective immediately. A wide horizon, the size of a tree or the rhythm of waves reminds you that life is bigger than your current worries. The scale of nature pulls you out of narrow focus. When you see yourself as part of something vast, everyday struggles lose their grip. Make it a habit to pause and look at the sky, watch water move or listen to wind in the leaves. These simple acts reconnect you to a larger story. This practice reduces anxiety and builds calm. Nature does not solve your problems, but it reshapes how you carry them. That shift is often enough to lighten the weight and give you renewed strength to continue.

90. Move your body outdoors

Exercise is powerful on its own, but pairing movement with nature multiplies the effect. A run in the park, yoga on the grass or even a slow walk by trees engages your senses while strengthening your body. The combination of physical effort and natural environment boosts mood, sharpens focus and reduces stress faster than indoor routines alone. Nature turns ordinary exercise into a source of energy and calm. You do not need perfection or long hours. Even short sessions outside can shift your day. By moving outdoors regularly, you create a ritual that benefits both body and mind. This habit builds resilience, making you feel stronger, clearer and more alive. Nature becomes not just a backdrop but an active partner in your well-being.

Forgive and Move On

Forgive and Move On:
Lightening the weight you carry

Holding on to anger feels powerful at first, but over time it drains you. Resentment takes energy, clouds judgment and keeps you tied to moments you wish had never happened. Forgiveness is often misunderstood as saying that what happened was acceptable. In truth, it is not about excusing others but about freeing yourself. By choosing to forgive, you stop allowing the past to decide how you feel today. Forgiveness is not a gift to the other person, it is a gift to yourself. The process is not quick or easy. It requires patience and a willingness to face pain without letting it define you. Forgiveness does not erase memory, but it softens its hold. It opens space for peace where bitterness once lived. Each step toward forgiveness makes life lighter, because you are no longer carrying the same heavy load. Eventually, he act of letting go turns into strength. It shows you that healing is possible, that you can move forward without being chained to the past.

*"Forgiveness is the fragrance
that the violet sheds on the heel
that has crushed it."
– Mark Twain*

91. Begin with forgiving yourself

The hardest forgiveness is often the one directed inward. Many people replay their own mistakes for years, holding themselves to impossible standards. This constant self-blame creates shame that blocks growth. The first step is to recognize that errors are part of being human. Write down what you still punish yourself for and ask honestly: does carrying this guilt help me improve or does it only keep me stuck? More often than not, it keeps you stuck. Self-forgiveness is not forgetting, it is choosing to learn instead of staying trapped. By treating yourself with compassion, you give yourself permission to try again. This inner kindness builds strength and resilience. When you forgive yourself, you stop being your own jailer and start being your own ally.

92. Release the story you repeat

Resentment survives because of repetition. You tell yourself the same story of how you were wronged and with each retelling, the pain grows sharper. Forgiveness begins when you interrupt that cycle. Instead of focusing on what was done to you, shift attention to what you want now. Ask: what future am I building and how is this old story holding me back? When you stop rehearsing the pain, you create room for healing. This does not mean pretending nothing happened, it means refusing to let the same wound dictate every day. By loosening the story, you loosen its grip. Over time, you find yourself thinking less about the past and more about what lies ahead. That is when real freedom begins.

93. Turn forgiveness into freedom

Forgiveness is not about pretending the hurt never happened and it is not about letting someone escape responsibility. It is about reclaiming your own life. Carrying anger keeps you tied to the moment of pain, as if it were still happening. Every time you replay the memory, you allow that wound to steal part of your present. Forgiveness breaks that chain. It does not erase the past, but it removes its power to control your future. Choosing to forgive means you stop reliving the same injury and begin living your own story again. The process takes patience. Begin by acknowledging the full weight of what happened. Do not minimize it, but do not let it define you either. Write about it, talk about it or reflect on it until the truth is clear. Then move toward release. You are not forgiving because the other person deserves it. You are forgiving because you deserve peace. Every time bitterness rises, remind yourself that holding on harms you more than it harms them.

As you practice, the release becomes real. The memory stays, but the emotional charge fades. You begin to notice that you can think of the event without being consumed by anger. That shift is freedom. It opens a space where joy can return and where new experiences can take root. Forgiveness does not make you weak. It shows your strength, because you chose healing over hatred. In letting go, you prove to yourself that you are stronger than what once wounded you. Forgiveness also teaches you that your well-being does not depend on another person's apology. By choosing release, you reclaim control over your own story.

Surround Yourself With Inspiration

Surround Yourself With Inspiration: Fuel for your spirit

What you surround yourself with shapes how you think and feel. If your environment is dull or draining, your energy sinks with it. Inspiration, on the other hand, is fuel. It sparks new ideas, lifts your mood and reminds you of possibilities you might have forgotten. Inspiration does not arrive by accident, it grows from what you choose to let in. When you fill your space and your life with uplifting influences, you create an atmosphere where creativity and motivation thrive. Inspiration can come from many places. A book that changes how you see the world, music that shifts your emotions, art that makes you pause or conversations with people who energize you. Even small details, like a quote on your wall or a podcast on your walk, can act as sparks. The key is to notice what lifts you and to invite more of it into your daily routine. These choices accumulate into an environment that keeps you moving forward. By surrounding yourself with inspiration, you give yourself a constant reminder that life is bigger than the moment you are in and that there is always more to learn, create and become.

"Inspiration exists, but it has to find you working."
- Pablo Picasso

94. Curate what you see every day

Your environment constantly shapes your mindset, often without you noticing. If your space is cluttered or uninspiring, your energy reflects that. Start curating what surrounds you. Hang art or photos that make you feel alive, place books where you can reach them or add colors that lift your mood. Even small adjustments, like a plant on your desk or a meaningful object in sight, can change how a day feels. When you choose what you look at, you choose what your mind absorbs. Inspiration is not only about grand gestures but about daily reminders that beauty, growth and creativity belong in your life. A curated environment becomes a silent coach, keeping you motivated without words.

95. Spend time with inspiring people

The people you choose to spend time with shape your mood, your thoughts and even your goals. If your circle is filled with negativity, it becomes harder to stay motivated. If it is filled with people who dream, create and push themselves, you are pulled upward with them. Make space for those who encourage you, who share ideas and who challenge you to see yourself differently. These people do not need to be famous or extraordinary. Sometimes they are friends who never give up, mentors who speak honestly or colleagues who bring passion to their work. Inspiring people expand your sense of possibility and reflect back strengths you forget you have. By surrounding yourself with such company, you build an atmosphere where growth feels natural and where motivation has room to breathe.

96. Collect sparks from the world

Inspiration is not a rare gift reserved for special moments. It is everywhere, woven into the fabric of daily life, waiting for you to notice. The problem is not a lack of inspiration but a lack of attention. When you slow down, the world offers countless sparks: the way shadows stretch across a street in the late afternoon, the scent of bread from a bakery the pattern of leaves pressed against a window after rain. These details may seem ordinary, yet when you pause to take them in, they carry surprising energy. Noticing beauty in overlooked places turns everyday life into a source of creativity. Make it a habit to collect these sparks. Carry a notebook, use your phone or keep a box of mementos. Write down phrases that strike you, sketch shapes you see or save colors and textures that catch your eye. These fragments form a personal archive of inspiration. On days when motivation runs low, looking back at them reignites your energy. In the process, you begin to trust that inspiration is not something you must chase, it is always around you.

The key is curiosity. Instead of waiting for big breakthroughs, approach the world as if everything has something to teach you. Try listening closely to the rhythm of a city, paying attention to the colors in a crowded market or noticing how music changes your mood. Each spark becomes fuel for your creativity, not because it solves problems directly, but because it shifts how you see. The more you collect, the more you realize that inspiration is less about luck and more about training your eyes and heart to stay open.

Stay Open to Change

Stay Open to Change:
Keeping your spark alive

Change can feel unsettling, because it forces you out of routines that feel safe. Yet nothing ages the mind faster than clinging to the way things used to be. When you resist change, you shrink your world. When you stay open to it, you expand. Openness does not mean you love every shift or that you never feel fear. It means you are willing to learn, adapt and try again. Flexibility is the real fountain of youth, because it keeps you curious, capable,and alive. Life never stands still. Technology evolves, friendships shift and your own goals change shape. Fighting that truth only creates tension. Embracing it gives you freedom. Staying open is about asking: what can this new chapter teach me? Each change, even when difficult, carries lessons and opportunities that make you stronger. The more you lean into this mindset, the lighter you feel. Instead of dreading the future, you begin to look forward to it. Change becomes proof that you are still growing, still moving, still alive.

"The measure of intelligence is the ability to change."
– Albert Einstein

97. Welcome small shifts daily

Change does not always arrive as a life-altering event. Often it comes in small doses: a different recipe or a conversation with someone outside your usual circle. These shifts may seem trivial, yet they train your mind to adapt without resistance. The more you practice adjusting in small ways, the less intimidating bigger changes feel. Treat daily life as a playground for flexibility. Rearrange your furniture, try a hobby for a week or read a genre you usually avoid. Each small shift reminds you that you are capable of learning and adapting at any age. This habit creates momentum, showing you that change is not a threat but a chance to expand. With time, you stop clinging to sameness and start welcoming variety as proof that you are still evolving.

98. Reframe uncertainty as possibility

Uncertainty often feels like the enemy of comfort. When you do not know what is coming, you imagine the worst. But uncertainty also means the future is not fixed, which makes it full of potential. The same unknown that scares you also carries surprises, opportunities and new paths you cannot yet see. Begin by shifting your language. Instead of saying "I do not know what will happen," try "I wonder what might happen." This small change turns fear into curiosity. When you reframe uncertainty as possibility, you loosen the grip of fear. This practice transforms how you face the unknown. You stop bracing for disaster and start expecting discovery. That mindset makes you more resilient, because you see the future not as a threat but as an invitation.

99. Make change your lifelong companion

Most people spend their lives resisting change, wishing things could stay as they are. Yet the only constant in life is movement. The world shifts, people evolve, seasons turn and you are part of that same flow. Fighting it only creates exhaustion. Embracing it gives you freedom. To stay open to change, think of it not as a disruption but as a companion that walks beside you. When change arrives, instead of asking "Why me?" try asking "What can this teach me?" That small shift in language turns fear into possibility. Change is not the enemy of stability, it is the source of growth. One way to practice is to look back at your life so far. Every major step forward happened because something shifted: a job ended, a friendship transformed, an unexpected opportunity appeared. At the time, you may have felt fear or even loss, yet those moments shaped who you are today. Let them remind you that new chapters often hide gifts you cannot see at first. The challenge is to trust the process long enough to discover them.

Openness also means curiosity. Try things without needing guarantees. Join a class in a subject you know nothing about, explore a new city without a map or speak with someone whose life looks different from yours. Each act of openness is like a muscle rep that keeps your spirit flexible. Over time, change stops feeling like an intruder and starts feeling like a partner. You realize that staying open is not just about surviving shifts but about thriving because of them. The choice to remain flexible is what keeps you young, alive and ready for whatever comes next.

Legendary, Not Ordinary

You're Not Done Yet, You're Just Getting Started

So here you are, standing at the end of this book. You made it through every page, every laugh, every reminder that life doesn't stop being fun, bold or ridiculous just because you've collected a few more birthdays. If anything, this is where it really begins. Age is not a countdown, it's an upgrade. Every year adds layers of experience, humor, resilience and a sharper sense of what actually matters. That is not decline, that is power.

Forget the cliché of the grumpy old woman shaking her fist at the world. That's not your path. You've laughed too hard, loved too deeply and learned too much to spend your life bitter at the sidelines. You are not fading into the background. You are stepping into your prime. The so-called "good years" are not behind you, they are right now and they stretch ahead waiting to be claimed. You are not small, you are not done and you are certainly not invisible.

Here is the truth: nobody remembers the woman who played it safe, who stayed quiet, who kept her sparkle hidden. People remember the ones who dared to live loudly, who spoke their mind, who kept saying yes to adventure when everyone else was retreating. That is you. The world doesn't need you toned down. It needs you in full color, with your quirks, your humor, your ideas and your unstoppable spirit.

So what comes next? Anything you want. Start a new chapter. Reinvent yourself. Travel, write, create, love, learn, rest or dance in your kitchen at midnight just because you can. Your story isn't shrinking, it's expanding. The future is not closing in, it's opening wide.

And remember this: You are not grumpy. You are legendary. Your best chapters are not behind you. They are waiting for you to write them.

Acknowledgments

Thank you for reading this book. We created it with care, humor and a lot of love for the idea that life only gets richer when you keep your spark alive. Our hope is that it gave you not just laughs but also moments that stay with you long after you close these pages.

If you have questions, feedback or simply want to share your thoughts, feel free to reach us at contact@bergmann-publishing.com. We always enjoy hearing from readers and believe that every story, including yours, adds to the bigger conversation about how to live fully and joyfully.

Thanks again for spending your time with us. May you keep finding new ways to stay bold, curious and unapologetically legendary!

König-Bergmann Publishing

Idea and writing: Cheryl Howley
Illustrations: Anna Parker

105 Albert Palace Mansions, Lurline Gardens
London SW11 4DH
United Kingdom

contact@bergmann-publishing.com

Made in the USA
Middletown, DE
24 February 2026